Fur, Feathers, HAIR

Fur, Feathers,
HAIR

By **Marguerite Rush Lerner, M.D.**

Illustrated by **Betty Sievert**

MEDICAL BOOKS FOR CHILDREN
LERNER PUBLICATIONS COMPANY
MINNEAPOLIS, MINNESOTA

International Copyright Secured. Printed in U.S.A.

Standard Book Number: 8225-0014-0
Library of Congress Catalog Card Number: 62-16851

Second Printing 1963
Third Printing 1966
Fourth Printing 1967
Fifth Printing 1968
Sixth Printing 1969

Contents

CHAPTER I

Animals 6

What is hair? 8
Why animals need hair 10
To keep us warm 13
How does hair grow? 15

CHAPTER II

Birds 16

What are feathers? 16
Molting 18
If you had a feather 20

CHAPTER III

People 22

Human hair 22
What's inside? 25
Permanent waves 26
Bare heads 29
Cutting and shaving 30
Goose pimples 30
A dozen facts about hair 31

CHAPTER I

Animals

If birds have feathers and animals have fur, what do people have on top of their skin? Hair, of course.

Some people have hair that is straight as a stick. Others have hair curled tight as a spring or softly waved. Hair can be black, brown, red, yellow or a mixture of colors. Did you ever hear of a towhead? That is a name given to a person with hair so blond that it looks white.

Hair may be thick or thin, coarse or fine. Sometimes there is no hair at all!

Most people, and many animals, have hair. All birds have feathers. Feathers, fur, wool, hair — even the porcupine's quills — are made of the same chemical material.

Animals need their hair. People do not. Head hair is an ornament that we brush and comb because it looks better that way. Why do girls let their hair grow? Are they trying to keep their ears warm? No. They want long hair because it is pretty. But animals and birds need their hair or feathers to protect them from cold and hot weather, sunlight and rain.

What is hair?

Hair is a *fiber* (FYE-bur). It is tough like thread. It grows out of a small pit in the skin called a *follicle* (FOL-i-kul). Wool—the soft fur coat that keeps animals warm—is made up of millions of hair fibers.

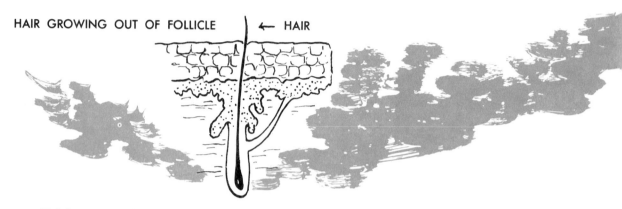

HAIR GROWING OUT OF FOLLICLE ← HAIR

Did you know that hair protects animals in cold weather just the way double walls *insulate,* or protect, a house?

In a house, the outside wall and the inside wall have air sandwiched between them. The trapped air *insulates* the house. It keeps the cold out and the heat in. Almost the same thing happens in an animal. Air gets caught between the hair fibers. The trapped air *insulates* the animal.

Why animals need hair

We know that animal hair makes a warm coat. But is it good for anything else?

The female rabbit builds her babies' nest with hair. For building materials she plucks hair from her body.

Hair color helps an animal hide from its enemies. The tiger's stripes and the leopard's spots are a good *camouflage* (CAM-o-flage). The hare that grows a white fur coat in the winter is hard to see in the snowy woods.

Not all animal hair is soft wool and fur. Some hairs are coarse and stiff. These are called *guard hairs*. The porcupine's armor of quills or spines is made of very large guard hairs. The hog's bristles that stand up when the hog is angry are guard hairs. The lion has a hairy mane which protects him against the claws of other animals. And the horse's tail is a built-in fly swatter!

Hairs that help the owner find out something are called *sensory* (SEN - sor - y) hairs. An animal may have them about the face. The cat's whiskers are hairy feelers. People, too, have hairs that act like antennae. Stiff fibers in the nose and ears warn you when an insect attacks. If dirt hits your eyelashes, the lids shut quickly to protect your eyes.

To keep us warm

Man is not born with a thick coat of wool, so he borrows hair from animals to keep warm. The bear, beaver, camel, fox, lamb, mink, otter, rabbit, raccoon, seal and squirrel are some of the animals whose fur has been made into warm and beautiful coats for men and women. Can you think of other animal fur that makes good coats?

People have invented fibers to take the place of animal hair. Nylon, Orlon and Acrilon are a few of the man-made fibers that are very useful.

For many years the best material for warm clothing came from *fleece*. Fleece is the thick wool that covers sheep.

The fleece we use is wool from ordinary sheep. Wool is valuable because it is warm without being heavy and is also very elastic. Wool gives warmth by trapping air which acts as insulation.

Wool fibers grow out of pits or follicles in the skin just the way ordinary hairs do. Yet they are different. They are made of tiny pieces or scales which lap over one another so that the fibers hook together. Wool is curly. For every inch of wool fiber, there are from 6 to 24 curls. Pull the fiber straight, and it springs right back into shape when you let it go.

A full-grown Merino sheep has from 30,000 to 50,000 fibers in every square inch of fleece. This is about 126 million fibers altogether. The sheep gets a haircut about once a year. If the fleece is not clipped for a few years, the fibers may grow more than a yard long.

MERINO SHEEP

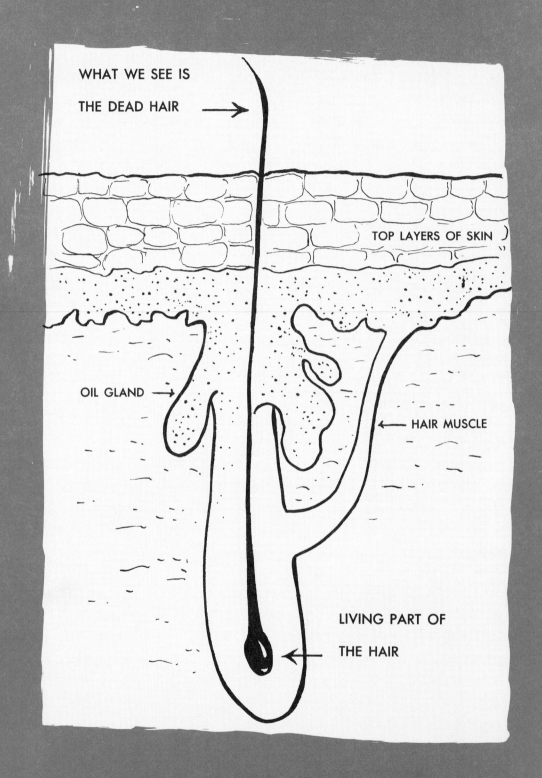

WHAT WE SEE IS

THE DEAD HAIR →

TOP LAYERS OF SKIN

OIL GLAND →

← HAIR MUSCLE

LIVING PART OF

THE HAIR ←

How does hair grow?

Man's hair does not grow forever. It grows in *cycles* (SY - kuls).

First, a hair forms at the bottom of the pit or hair follicle deep in the skin. The hair grows for awhile and then stops. After this resting stage another new hair forms in the same place. The old hair is pushed out by the new one. The *shaft* of the hair that sticks out of the skin is dead. The living part of the hair is the onion-shaped *bulb* deep inside the skin.

In many animals all the hair follicles work together. They all grow new hairs or rest quietly at the same time. The mouse, rat and rabbit are some of the animals that grow new hair all over the body at the same time.

In a small number of animals the hair follicles do not rest. The hair grows constantly. This is what happens in the angora rabbit and some kinds of sheep, goats, pigs and cats. The long, fine, silky wool from angora rabbits makes fuzzy mittens, scarfs and sweaters.

In man, and in some animals such as the guinea pig and cat, the hair follicles do not work together at the same time. One follicle may form a hair while another one rests. Because some hairs are growing all the time, people do not *molt* or shed their hair the way ducks cast off feathers.

Hair on the head grows the longest. This happens because follicles on the scalp work for several years but rest for only a few months. There are so many follicles on the head — about 100 thousand — that it seems as if scalp hair is growing all the time. Some women have hair a yard long!

If an animal is born without hair follicles, or if the follicles are destroyed, no hair can grow. That is why you sometimes see cats, dogs, pigs, sheep and other animals without hair. When people do not have hair, they are said to be *bald*.

CHAPTER II

Birds

What are feathers?

Birds are different from all other animals because they have feathers. Feathers, like hair, grow out of follicles in the skin.

A feather is a shaft or stem with hairy side branches called *barbs*. The short part of the feather that is sunk into the skin is the *quill*. The quill is hollow like a tube.

A bird has three types of feathers. Those on the outside are *contour* (KON - toor) feathers. They form the shape of the bird's body and tail and are needed for flying.

At the bottom of the contour feathers are *filoplumes* (FY - lo - plooms) which look like tiny tufts of thread.

Hiding way underneath are soft, fluffy *down* feathers.

WING FEATHER

← FILOPLUMES

← QUILL

UNDER FEATHER

DOWN FEATHER

Molting

When animals shed their skin, fur, or feathers, we say that they are *molting*. Baby snakes double in size and burst out in new skin before they reach their first birthday. Furry animals grow different coats for summer and winter. Birds exchange their worn out feathers for new ones.

Birds molt once or twice a year. New feathers grow in place of the old ones. Most birds still have enough power to fly after molting because they do not lose their feathers all at once. Instead, the flight feathers drop off two at a time, one on each side.

Many water birds cast off all their flight feathers at the same time. Ducks and geese do this and cannot fly for awhile. They have to wait until they grow new flight feathers.

Penguins, too, lose all their feathers at once. But it is not molting that keeps penguins grounded. Their stiff wings do not bend like those of other birds and are better for paddling water than for flapping air. Penguins are good swimmers, but they cannot fly.

Birds need their feathers for warmth, flying, hiding from enemies and attracting mates. Feathers are good egg warmers, and they keep newly hatched birds snug and safe.

If you had a feather

What would you do with a
feather? Stick it in a hat? Dip it
in ink? Save it for a friend?

Feathers are fun to play with.
They also are useful. Feathers are
collected from nests when the
young birds no longer need them.
Or they are plucked from living
birds in the spring. When a feather
is plucked, a new one forms in
the follicle.

Feathers are soft, elastic and light.
That is why they are good for filling
mattresses and cushions. Chicken
feathers are coarser than those from
water birds like ducks, geese and
swans. Downy feathers from the
Eider duck make very soft pillows.
The female duck plucks the down
from her body to line the nest for
her babies.

Quill pens are often made from goose feathers. Only the five outer wing feathers are useful. A right-handed person should choose a left wing feather, and a left-handed person should choose a right wing feather. It is easier to write with a quill that curves outward and away from the writer. George Washington, Benjamin Franklin and all the other signers of the Declaration of Independence wrote with quill pens.

Feather money is used in some Pacific Islands. Downy red feathers, plucked from a tropical forest bird, are glued together to form a belt. A new piece of red-feather money is worth about $56 in the Santa Cruz Islands.

Feathers make colorful ornaments. Knights wore plumes in their helmets. North American Indians put eagle feathers around their heads. Ostrich feathers are cleaned, curled and dyed to decorate women's hats. A man's hat often has a small peacock, pheasant or parrot feather on it.

CHAPTER III
People

Human hair

Man has much less hair than his animal friends. Many thousands of years ago people had more hair on their bodies than now.

Before birth, human babies are covered with a silky coat of *primary* hair. This is shed while the baby is still inside the mother. When the baby is born, it has soft, downy *secondary* hair which is often called *lanugo* (la-NOO-go). It gets its name from *lana,* the Latin word for wool.

As a child grows, the fine baby hair, or lanugo, is exchanged for a slightly coarser hair. This is the light colored fuzz that is found all over the body.

The much thicker and darker hair of the head, beard, arms and legs is called *terminal* hair.

Sometimes, but not often, a person is born with long, fine hair covering his body. This happens by mistake if the primary hair is not shed. Years ago these people with long, silky coats of primary hair might join a circus and be called *dog men*.

Soon after birth most babies lose some hair over the front and back of the head. These are the same parts of the scalp that become bald in grown men. But baldness in babies occurs in both girls and boys and does not last long. Even while some hair is falling out, new hair is growing in. By the time most children are one or two years old, they have hair all over the scalp. Girls keep their hair for the rest of their lives. But many boys lose part of their scalp hair as they grow older.

While boys and girls are growing to adulthood, their hair becomes darker, thicker and stronger. After people reach the age of 35, their hair begins to lose its color and turn gray or white. When people are old their hair becomes thinner and breaks more easily.

There is no hair on the palms, the sides or ends of the fingers or on the bottom of the feet and toes.

What's inside?

Hair, fur and feathers are all made of the same stuff—a chemical called *keratin* (KER-a-tin). Keratin gets its name from the Greek words, *keras* and *keratos,* which mean horn. If there were no keratin, animals' horns and hoofs and even people's nails would be soft and weak instead of hard and strong.

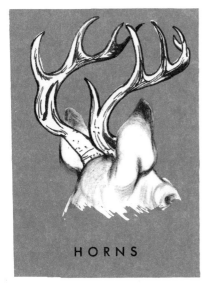

HORNS

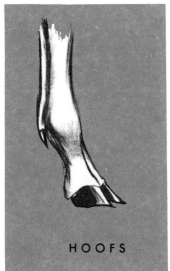

HOOFS

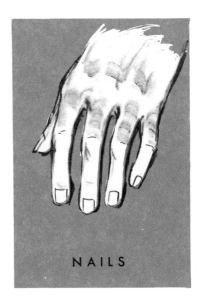

NAILS

Keratin is a *protein* (PRO-teen). There are many different kinds of proteins. In fact, much of our food contains proteins, especially meat, milk and eggs. But keratin is not the kind of protein one would choose to eat. It is too hard and does not taste very good.

It is keratin that makes hair very elastic. When you stretch hair, and let it go again, it springs back like a rubber band. It is easier to stretch wet hair than dry hair.

Permanent waves

Many women who have straight hair would rather have it curly. They can make it curly by using a *cold wave set.*

First the hair is washed. Then it is sponged with *thioglycollate* (thy-o-GLY-ko-late). This is a special chemical that stretches the hair even more than it can be stretched with water. The stretched hair is combed into curls or waves. Then the thioglycollate is removed by rinsing the hair with water. When the hair dries, it is wavy. This is called a *permanent wave,* but it really isn't permanent because it lasts only until the hair grows longer and is cut.

Bare heads

After the age of 20, men may get *common baldness*. Women do not. This occurs only in some men who have baldness in their families.

The hair becomes thinner and makes an M-shaped pattern at the front of the scalp. Sometimes the whole head looks bare.

The hair is not actually lost. Instead, the hair follicles shrink in size and produce hair that is short, fine and light colored—like baby hair. It is not possible to correct the hair follicles in common baldness.

There are other types of hair changes.

If a person has been sick with a high fever, the hair may fall out after a few months. During illness, the hair follicles rest longer. And resting hairs fall out more easily than growing hairs.

Germs, especially *fungi* (FUN - jee), may attack growing hairs and make them break off.

In some women the scalp hair becomes thinner after they have a baby. Later the hair grows back.

Round, bald spots may appear in the scalp of males or females at any age. These hairless circles are not a form of common baldness. Usually the hair grows back.

Cutting and shaving

Cutting and shaving do not make hair grow faster or thicker. Immediately after shaving, hair grows a little more quickly for a short time. But right after this spurt, the hair grows more slowly. The fast rate is cancelled out by the slow one. By the end of a day the hair is exactly as long as if it hadn't been shaved at all.

Goose pimples

When people are cold or frightened, they get *goose pimples*. These are little bumps in the skin caused by the pulling of tiny muscles attached to the hair roots. The same type of muscle pull in animals makes guard hairs stand up or bristle.

A DOZEN FACTS ABOUT HAIR

1. Hair grows faster during the day than at night.

2. Hair grows faster and longer in the summer than in the winter.

3. Hair on the head and chin grows the fastest and longest.

4. A single scalp hair grows ½ inch a month.

5. Hair grows slowest on the eyebrows, eyelashes and legs.

6. Hair in the armpits grows almost as fast as that on the scalp.

7. Scalp hair grows faster in women than in men.

8. Armpit hair grows faster in men than in women.

9. Eyebrows grow at the same speed in both men and women.

10. Scalp hair grows fastest when people are between 15 and 30 years old.

11. Hair cannot turn gray overnight—unless you dye the hair that color. It will turn gray by itself after a long time. This happens when special cells around the hair roots are no longer able to make pigment or coloring material.

12. If all the hair that your body makes in one day were placed end to end, you would have a hair chain about 100 feet long.

The human body is amazing. Producing hair
is one of the wonderful things it can do.

We specialize in publishing quality books for
young people. For a complete list please write

LERNER PUBLICATIONS COMPANY

241 First Avenue North, Minneapolis, Minnesota 55401